Perl 5
Desktop Reference

Perl 5
Desktop Reference

Johan Vromans

O'Reilly & Associates, Inc.
Cambridge   Köln   Paris   Sebastopol   Tokyo

Perl 5 Desktop Reference
by Johan Vromans

Copyright © 1996 Johan Vromans. All rights reserved. Printed
in the United States of America.

Cover design Copyright © 1996 O'Reilly & Associates, Inc. All
rights reserved. Printed in the United States of America.

Production Editor: Clairemarie Fisher O'Leary

Printing History:

February 1996: First Edition.

ISBN: 1-56592-187-9   [7/97]

Table of Contents

	Page
Conventions	1
Command-Line Options	1
Syntax	3
Literals	4
Variables	5
Operators and Precedence	7
Statements	8
Subroutines, Packages, and Modules	10
Pragmatic Modules	12
Object-Oriented Programming	13
Arithmetic Functions	13
Conversion Functions	14
Structure Conversion	15
String Functions	16
Array and Hash Functions	17
Regular Expressions	19
Search and Replace Functions	21
File Test Operators	23
File Operations	24
Input/Output	25
Formats	28
Directory Reading Routines	29
System Interaction	30
Networking	32
System V IPC	33
Miscellaneous	34
Information from System Files	35
Special Variables	37
Special Arrays	40

Standard Modules 41
Environment Variables 46
The Perl Debugger 46

Perl 5
Desktop Reference

Conventions

this	denotes text that you enter literally.
this	means variable text, i.e., things you must fill in.
this†	means that *this* will default to **$_** if omitted.
word	is a keyword, i.e., a word with a special meaning.
RETURN	denotes pressing a keyboard key.
[...]	denotes an optional part.

Command-Line Options

-a
turns on autosplit mode when used with **-n** or **-p**. Splits to **@F**.

-c
checks syntax but does not execute. It does run **BEGIN** and **END** blocks.

-d
runs the script under the debugger. Use **-de** 0 to start the debugger without a script.

-D *number*
sets debugging flags.

-e *commandline*
may be used to enter a single line of script. Multiple **-e** commands may be given to build up a multiline script.

-F *regexp*
specifies a regular expression to split on if **-a** is in effect.

-h	prints the Perl usage summary. Does not execute.
-i*ext*	files processed by the < > construct are to be edited in place.
-I*dir*	with -P, tells the C preprocessor where to look for include files. The directory is prepended to @INC.
-l [*octnum*]	
	enables automatic line-end processing, e.g., -l013.
-m *module*	
	imports the *module* before executing the script. *module* may be followed by a = and a comma-separated list of items.
-M *module*	
	same as -m, but with more trickery.
-n	assumes an input loop around your script. Lines are not printed.
-p	assumes an input loop around your script. Lines are printed.
-P	runs the C preprocessor on the script before compilation by Perl.
-s	interprets -xxx on the command line as a switch and sets the corresponding variable $xxx in the script.
-S	uses the **PATH** environment variable to search for the script.
-T	turns on taint checking.
-u	dumps core after compiling the script. To be used with the *undump*(1) program (where available).
-U	allows Perl to perform unsafe operations.
-v	prints the version and patchlevel of your Perl executable.
-V [:*var*]	
	prints Perl configuration information.
-w	prints warnings about possible spelling errors and other error-prone constructs in the script.

-x [*dir*]

extracts Perl program from the input stream. If *dir* is specified, switches to this directory before running the program.

-0 [*val*]

(that's the number zero.) Designates an initial value for the record separator $/. See also -l.

Syntax

Perl is a free-format programming language. This means that in general it does not matter how a Perl program is written with regard to indentation and lines.

An exception to this rule is when the Perl compiler encounters a sharp or pound symbol (#) in the input: it then discards this symbol and everything following it up to the end of the current input line. This can be used to put comments in Perl programs. Real programmers put lots of useful comments in their programs.

There are places where whitespace does matter: within literal texts, patterns and formats.

If the Perl compiler encounters the special token __END__, it discards this symbol and stops reading input. Anything following this token is ignored by the Perl compiler, but can be read by the program when it is run.

When the Perl compiler encounters a line that starts with =, it skips all input up to and including a line that starts with =cut. This is used to embed program documentation.

Literals

Numeric

> **123 1_234 123.4 5E-10 0xff** (hex) **0377** (octal)

String **'abc'**

> literal string, no variable interpolation or escape
> characters, except **\'** and ****. Also: **q/abc/**. Almost
> any pair of delimiters can be used instead of **/.../**.

"abc"

> Variables are interpolated and escape sequences are
> processed. Also: **qq/abc/**.
>
> Escape sequences: **\t** (Tab), **\n** (Newline),
> **\r** (Return), **\f** (Formfeed), **\b** (Backspace),
> **\a** (Alarm), **\e** (Escape), **\033** (octal), **\x1b** (hex),
> **\c[** (control).
>
> **\l** and **\u** lowercase/uppercase the following charac-
> ter. **\L** and **\U** lowercase/uppercase until a **\E** is
> encountered. **\Q** quotes regular expression charac-
> ters until a **\E** is encountered.

`command`

> evaluates to the output of the *command*. Also:
> **qx/***command***/**.

Boolean

> Perl has no boolean data type. Anything that evalu-
> ates to the null string, the number zero, or the string
> "0" is considered **false**, everything else is **true** (includ-
> ing strings like "00"!).

Array   (1, 2, 3) three-member array.

> ( ) empty array.
> (1..4) is the same as (1,2,3,4),
> likewise ('a'..'z').
> **qw/foo bar** .../ is the same as ('foo','bar',...).

Array reference

> [1,2,3]

Hash (associative array)

        (*key1*, *val1*, *key2*, *val2*, ...)

        Also (*key1* => *val1*, *key2* => *val2*, ...)

Hash reference

        {*key1*, *val1*, *key2*, *val2*, ...}

Code reference

        sub { *statements* }

Filehandles

        STDIN, **STDOUT**, **STDERR**, **ARGV**, **DATA**.

        User-specified: *handle*, $*var*.

Globs   <*pattern*> evaluates to all filenames according to the pattern. Use <${*var*}> or **glob** $*var* to glob from a variable.

Here–Is <<*identifier*

        Shell-style "here document." See the Perl manual for details.

Special tokens

        __FILE__: filename; __LINE__: line number;

        __END__: end of program; remaining lines can be read using the filehandle **DATA**.

Variables

$**var**   a simple scalar variable.

$**var**[28]

        29th element of array @**var**.

$**p** = \@**var**

        now $**p** is a reference to array @**var**.

$$**p**[28]

        29th element of array referenced by $**p**.

        Also, $**p**->[28].

$**var**[-1]

        last element of array @**var**.

$**var**[$**i**][$**j**]

        $**j**-th element of $**i**-th element of array @**var**.

$var{'Feb'}
> a value from hash (associative array) %var.

$p = \%var
> now $p is a reference to hash %var.

$$p{'Feb'}
> a value from hash referenced by $p.
> Also, $p->{'Feb'}.

$#var   last index of array @var.

@var   the entire array; in a scalar context, the number of elements in the array.

@var[3,4,5]
> a slice of array @var.

@var{'a','b'}
> a slice of %var; same as ($var{'a'},$var{'b'}).

%var   the entire hash; in a scalar context, true if the hash has elements.

$var{'a',1,...}
> emulates a multidimensional array.

('a'...'z')[4,7,9]
> a slice of an array literal.

pkg::*var* a variable from a package, e.g., **$pkg::var**, **@pkg::ary**.

*thingie*** reference to a thingie, e.g., **\$var**, **\%hash**.

name* refers to all thingies represented by *name*.
> ***n1 = *n2** makes **n1** an alias for **n2**.
> ***n1 = $n2** makes **$n1** an alias for **$n2**.

You can always use a { *block* } returning the right type of reference instead of the variable identifier, e.g., **${...}**, **&{...}**. **$$p** is just a shorthand for **${$p}**.

Operators and Precedence

Perl operators have the following associativity and precedence, listed from highest precedence to lowest.

Assoc.	Operators	Description
left	terms and list operators	See below
left	->	Infix dereference operator
	++ --	Auto-increment (magical on strings) Auto-decrement
right	**	Exponentiation
right right right	\\ ! ~ + -	Reference to an object (unary) Unary negation, bitwise complement Unary plus, minus
left left	=~ !~	Binds a scalar expression to a pattern match Same, but negates the result
left	* / % x	Multiplication, division, modulo, repetition
left	+ - .	Addition, subtraction, concatenation
left	>> <<	Bitwise shift right, bitwise shift left
	named unary operators	e.g. sin, chdir, -f, -M.
	< > <= >= lt gt le ge	Numerical relational operators String relational operators
	== != <=> eq ne cmp	Numerical equal, not equal, compare Stringwise equal, not equal, compare Compare operators return -1 (less), 0 (equal), or 1 (greater)
left	&	Bitwise AND
left	| ^	Bitwise OR, exclusive OR
left	&&	Logical AND
left	||	Logical OR
	..	In scalar context, range operator In array context, enumeration
right	?:	Conditional (if ? then : else) operator
right	= += -= etc.	Assignment operators

Assoc.	Operators	Description
left	,	Comma operator, also list element separator
left	=>	Same, enforces the left operand to be a string
	list operators (rightward)	See below
right	not	Low precedence logical NOT
left	and	Low precedence logical AND
left	or xor	Low precedence logical OR, exclusive OR

Parentheses can be used to group an expression into a term.

A list consists of expressions, variables, or lists, separated by commas. An array variable or an array slice may always be used instead of a list.

All Perl functions can be used as list operators, in which case they have very high or very low precedence, depending on whether you look at the left side of the operator or at the right side of the operator. Parentheses can be added around the parameter lists to avoid precedence problems.

The logical operators do not evaluate the right operand if the result is already known after evaluation of the left operand.

Statements

Every statement is an expression, optionally followed by a modifier, and terminated with a semicolon. The semicolon may be omitted if the statement is the final one in a *block*.

Execution of expressions can depend on other expressions using one of the modifiers if, unless, while, or until, e.g.:

    expr1 if expr2 ;
    expr1 until expr2 ;

The logical operators | |, &&, or ?: also allow conditional execution:

> *expr1* | | *expr2* ;
> *expr1* ? *expr2* : *expr3* ;

Statements can be combined to form a *block* when enclosed in {}. *block*s may be used to control flow:

> **if** (*expr*) *block* [[**elsif** (*expr*) *block*...] **else** *block*]
>
> **unless** (*expr*) *block* [**else** *block*]
>
> [*label*:] **while** (*expr*) *block* [**continue** *block*]
>
> [*label*:] **until** (*expr*) *block* [**continue** *block*]
>
> [*label*:] **for** ([*expr*] ; [*expr*] ; [*expr*]) *block*
>
> [*label*:] **foreach** *var*† (*list*) *block*
>
> [*label*:] *block* [**continue** *block*]

Program flow can be controlled with:

goto *label*

> Finds the statement labeled with *label* and resumes execution there. *label* may be an expression that evaluates to the name of a label.

last [*label*]

> Immediately exits the loop in question. Skips continue block.

next [*label*]

> Starts the next iteration of the loop.

redo [*label*]

> Restarts the loop block without evaluating the conditional again.

Special forms are:

> do *block* **while** *expr*;
> do *block* **until** *expr*;

which are guaranteed to perform *block* once before testing *expr*, and

> do *block*

which effectively turns *block* into an expression.

Subroutines, Packages, and Modules

&&*subroutine list*
> Executes a *subroutine* declared by a **sub** declaration, and returns the value of the last expression evaluated in *subroutine. subroutine* can be an expression yielding a reference to a code object. The **&** may be omitted if the subroutine has been declared before being used.

bless *ref* [, *classname*]
> Turns the object *ref* into an object in *classname*. Returns the reference.

caller [*expr*]
> Returns an array ($package, $file, $line,...) for a specific subroutine call. **caller** returns this information for the current subroutine, **caller(1)** for the caller of this subroutine, etc. Returns **false** if no caller.

do *subroutine list*
> Deprecated form of **&***subroutine* .

goto **&***subroutine*
> Substitutes a call to *subroutine* for the current subroutine.

import *module* [[*version*] *list*]
> Imports the named items from *module*.

no *module* [*list*]

>Cancels imported semantics. See **use**.

package *name*

>Designates the remainder of the current block as a package.

require *expr*†

>If *expr* is numeric, requires Perl to be at least that version. Otherwise *expr* must be the name of a file that is included from the Perl library. Does not include more than once, and yields a fatal error if the file does not evaluate to a **true** value. If *expr* is a bare word, assumes extension **.pm** for the name of the file. This form of loading of modules does not risk altering your namespace.

return *expr*

>Returns from a subroutine with the value specified.

sub *name* [(*proto*)] { *expr*; ...}

>Designates *name* as a subroutine. Parameters are passed by reference as array @_. Returns the value of the last expression evaluated. *proto* can be used to define the required parameters. Without a *block* it is just a forward declaration, without the *name* it is an anonymous subroutine.

[**sub**] **BEGIN** { *expr*; ...}

>Defines a setup *block* to be called before execution.

[**sub**] **END** { *expr*; ...}

>Defines a cleanup *block* to be called upon termination.

tie *var, classname,* [*list*]

>Ties a variable to a package class that will handle it. Can be used to bind a dbm or ndbm file to a hash.

tied *var* Returns a reference to the object underlying *var*, or the undefined value if *var* is not tied to a package class.

untie *var*

> Breaks the binding between the variable and the
> package class.

use *module* [[*version*] *list*]

> Imports semantics from the named module into the
> current package.

Pragmatic Modules

Pragmatic modules affect the compilation of your program.
Pragmatic modules can be activated (imported) with **use** and
deactivated with **no**. These are locally scoped.

diagnostics

> Force verbose warning diagnostics.

integer   Compute arithmetic in integer instead of double pre-
            cision.

less   Request less of something from the compiler.

lib   Manipulate @INC at compile time.

ops   Restrict unsafe operations when compiling.

overload   Package for overloading Perl operators.
            Example: **use overload "+" => \&my_add;**

sigtrap   Enable simple signal handling.
            Example: **use sigtrap qw(SEGV TRAP);**

strict   Restrict unsafe constructs.
            use strict "**refs**" restricts the use of symbolic refer-
            ences.
            use strict "**vars**" requires all variables to be either
            local or fully qualified.
            use strict "**subs**" restricts the use of bareword identif-
            iers that are not subroutines.

subs   Predeclare subroutine names, allowing you to use
            them without parentheses even before they are
            declared.
            Example: **use subs qw(ding dong);**

vars   Predeclare variable names, allowing you to use them under "use strict".
            Example: **use vars qw($foo @bar)**;

Object-Oriented Programming

Perl rules of object-oriented programming:

- An object is simply a reference that happens to know which class it belongs to. Objects are blessed, references are not.

- A class is simply a package that happens to provide methods to deal with object references. If a package fails to provide a method, the base classes as listed in **@ISA** are searched.

- A method is simply a subroutine that expects an object reference (or a package name, for static methods) as the first argument.

    Methods can be applied with:

    > *method objref parameters*   or
    > *objref–>method parameters*

Arithmetic Functions

abs *expr*†   Returns the absolute value of its operand.

atan2 *y*, *x*   Returns the arctangent of *y/x* in the range −π to π.

cos *expr*†   Returns the cosine of *expr* (expressed in radians).

exp *expr*†   Returns *e* to the power of *expr*.

int *expr*†   Returns the integer portion of *expr*.

log *expr*†   Returns natural logarithm (base *e*) of *expr*.

rand [*expr*]

            Returns a random fractional number between 0 and the value of *expr*. If *expr* is omitted, returns a value between 0 and 1.

sin *expr*†   Returns the sine of *expr* (expressed in radians).

sqrt *expr*†   Returns the square root of *expr*.

srand [*expr*]

    Sets the random number seed for the **rand** operator.

time   Returns the number of seconds since January 1, 1970. Suitable for feeding to **gmtime** and **localtime**.

Conversion Functions

chr *expr*†

    Returns the character represented by the decimal value *expr*.

gmtime *expr*†

    Converts a time as returned by the **time** function to a 9-element array (0:$sec, 1:$min, 2:$hour, 3:$mday, 4:$mon, 5:$year, 6:$wday, 7:$yday, 8:$isdst) with the time localized for the standard Greenwich time zone.

    $mon has the range 0..11 and $wday has the range 0..6.

hex *expr*†

    Returns the decimal value of *expr* interpreted as a hex string.

localtime *expr*†

    Converts a time as returned by the **time** function to *ctime*(3) string. In array context, returns a 9-element array with the time localized for the local time zone.

oct *expr*†

    Returns the decimal value of *expr* interpreted as an octal string. If *expr* starts off with **0x**, interprets it as a hex string instead.

ord *expr*†

    Returns the ASCII value of the first character of *expr*.

vec *expr, offset, bits*

> Treats string *expr* as a vector of unsigned integers of *bits* bits each, and yields the decimal value of the element at *offset. bits* must be a power of 2 between 1 and 32. May be assigned to.

Structure Conversion

pack *template, list*

> Packs the values into a binary structure using *template.*

unpack *template, expr*

> Unpacks the structure *expr* into an array, using *template.*

template is a sequence of characters as follows:

a	/	A	ASCII string, null- / space-padded
b	/	B	Bit string in ascending / descending order
c	/	C	Native / unsigned char value
f	/	d	Single / double float in native format
h	/	H	Hex string, low / high nybble first
i	/	I	Signed / unsigned integer value
l	/	L	Signed / unsigned long value
n	/	N	Short / long in network (big endian) byte order
s	/	S	Signed / unsigned short value
u	/	p	Uuencoded string / pointer to a string
P			Pointer to a structure (fixed-length string)
v	/	V	Short / long in VAX (little endian) byte order
x	/	@	Null byte / null fill until position
X			Backup a byte

Each character may be followed by a decimal number that will be used as a repeat count; an asterisk (*) specifies all remaining arguments. If the format is preceded with %*n*, **unpack** returns an *n*-bit checksum instead. Spaces may be included in the template for readability purposes.

String Functions

chomp *list*†

Removes line endings from all elements of the list; returns the (total) number of characters removed.

chop *list*†

Chops off the last character on all elements of the list; returns the last chopped character.

crypt *plaintext, salt*

Encrypts a string.

eval *expr*†

expr is parsed and executed as if it were a Perl program. The value returned is the value of the last expression evaluated. If there is a syntax error or runtime error, an undefined string is returned by **eval**, and $@ is set to the error message. See also **eval** in the section "Miscellaneous."

index *str, substr* [, *offset*]

Returns the position of *substr* in *str* at or after *offset*. If the substring is not found, returns −1 (but see $[in the section "Special Variables").

length *expr*†

Returns the length in characters of *expr*.

lc *expr*   Returns a lowercase version of *expr*.

lcfirst *expr*

Returns *expr* with its first character lowercase.

quotemeta *expr*

Returns *expr* with all regular expression metacharacters quoted.

rindex *str, substr* [, *offset*]

Returns the position of the last *substr* in *str* at or before *offset*.

substr *expr, offset* [, *len*]

Extracts a substring of length *len* out of *expr* and returns it. If *offset* is negative, counts from the end of

the string. If *len* is negative, leaves that many characters off the end of the string. May be assigned to.

uc *expr*   Returns an uppercase version of *expr*.

ucfirst *expr*

>Returns *expr* with its first character uppercase.

Array and Hash Functions

delete $*hash*{*key*}

>Deletes the specified value from the specified hash.
>Returns the deleted value (unless *hash* is tied to a
>package that does not support this).

each %*hash*

>Returns a 2-element array consisting of the key and
>value for the next value of the hash. Entries are
>returned in an apparently random order. After all
>values of the hash have been returned, an empty list
>is returned. The next call to each after that will start
>iterating again.

exists *expr*†

>Checks if the specified hash key exists in its hash
>array.

grep *expr*, *list*

grep *block list*

>Evaluates *expr* or *block* for each element of the *list*,
>locally setting $_ to refer to the element. Modifying
>$_ will modify the corresponding element from *list*.
>Returns the array of elements from *list* for which
>*expr* returned true.

join *expr*, *list*

>Joins the separate strings of *list* into a single string
>with fields separated by the value of *expr*, and
>returns the string.

keys %*hash*

>Returns an array of all the keys of the named hash.

map *expr*, *list*

map *block* *list*

> Evaluates *expr* or *block* for each element of the *list*,
> locally setting $_ to refer to the element. Modifying
> $_ will modify the corresponding element from *list*.
> Returns the list of results.

pop [@*array*]

> Pops off and returns the last value of the array. If
> @*array* is omitted, pops @**ARGV** in main and @_ in
> subroutines.

push @*array*, *list*

> Pushes the values of the *list* onto the end of the
> array.

reverse *list*

> In array context, returns the *list* in reverse order. In
> scalar context, returns the first element of *list* with
> bytes reversed.

scalar @*array*

> Returns the number of elements in the array.

scalar %*hash*

> Returns a true value if the hash has elements
> defined.

shift [@*array*]

> Shifts the first value of the array off and returns it,
> shortening the array by 1 and moving everything
> down. If @*array* is omitted, shifts @**ARGV** in main
> and @_ in subroutines.

sort [*subroutine*] *list*

> Sorts the *list* and returns the sorted array value. *sub-*
> *routine*, if specified, must return less than zero,
> zero, or greater than zero, depending on how the
> elements of the array (available to the routine as
> package global variables $**a** and $**b**) are to be
> ordered. *subroutine* may be the name of a user-
> defined routine, or a *block*.

splice @*array, offset* [, *length* [, *list*]]

> Removes the elements of @*array* designated by *offset* and *length*, and replaces them with *list* (if specified). Returns the elements removed.

split [*pattern* [, *expr*† [, *limit*]]]

> Splits *expr* (a string) into an array of strings, and returns it. If *limit* is specified, splits into at most that number of fields. If *pattern* is omitted, splits at the whitespace (after skipping any leading whitespace). If not in array context, returns number of fields and splits to @_. See also the section called "Search and Replace Functions."

unshift @*array, list*

> Prepends *list* to the front of the array, and returns the number of elements in the new array.

values %*hash*

> Returns a normal array consisting of all the values of the named hash.

Regular Expressions

Each character matches itself, unless it is one of the special characters + ? . * ^ $ ( ) [ ] { } | \. The special meaning of these characters can be escaped using a \.

.   matches an arbitrary character, but not a newline unless the \s modifier is used (see m//s).

(...)   groups a series of pattern elements to a single element.

^   matches the beginning of the target. In multiline mode (see m//m) also matches after every newline character.

$ matches the end of the line. In multiline mode also matches before every newline character.

[...]   denotes a class of characters to match. [^...] negates the class.

(... | ... | ...)

> matches one of the alternatives.

(?# *text*)

> Comment.

(?: *regexp*)

> Like (*regexp*) but does not make back-references.

(? = *regexp*)

> Zero width positive look-ahead assertion.

(?! *regexp*)

> Zero width negative look-ahead assertion.

(? *modifier*)

> Embedded pattern-match modifier. *modifier* can be one or more of i, m, s, or x.

Quantified subpatterns match as many times as possible. When followed with a ? they match the minimum number of times. These are the quantifiers:

+
: matches the preceding pattern element one or more times.

?
: matches zero or one times.

*
: matches zero or more times.

{*n,m*}
: denotes the minimum *n* and maximum *m* match count. {*n*} means exactly *n* times; {*n*,} means at least *n* times.

A \ escapes any special meaning of the following character if non-alphanumeric, but it turns most alphanumeric characters into something special:

\w
: matches alphanumeric, including _, \W matches non-alphanumeric.

\s
: matches whitespace, \S matches non-whitespace.

\d
: matches numeric, \D matches non-numeric.

\A
: matches the beginning of the string, \Z matches the end.

\b   matches word boundaries, **\B** matches non-boundaries.

\G   matches where the previous **m//g** search left off.

\n, \r, \f, \t, etc.

        have their usual meaning.

\w, \s, and **\d**

        may be used within character classes, **\b** denotes a backspace in this context.

Back-references:

\1…\9   refer to matched subexpressions, grouped with ( ), inside the match.

\10 and up

        can also be used if the pattern matches that many subexpressions.

See also **$1…$9, $+, $&, $`**, and **$'** in the section "Special Variables."

With modifier **x**, whitespace can be used in the patterns for readability purposes.

Search and Replace Functions

[*expr* =~] [m] /*pattern*/ [g] [i] [m] [o] [s] [x]

        Searches *expr* (default: $_) for a pattern. If you prepend an **m** you can use almost any pair of delimiters instead of the slashes. If used in array context, an array is returned consisting of the subexpressions matched by the parentheses in the pattern, i.e., (**$1, $2, $3,**…).

        Optional modifiers: **g** matches as many times as possible; **i** searches in a case-insensitive manner; **o** interpolates variables only once. **m** treats the string as multiple lines; **s** treats the string as a single line; **x** allows for regular expression extensions.

If *pattern* is empty, the most recent pattern from a previous successful match or replacement is used.

With **g** the match can be used as an iterator in scalar context.

?*pattern*?

This is just like the /*pattern*/ search, except that it matches only once between calls to the **reset** operator.

[$*var* =˜] s/*pattern*/*replacement*/ [e] [g] [i] [m] [o] [s] [x]

Searches a string for a pattern, and if found, replaces that pattern with the replacement text. It returns the number of substitutions made, if any; if no substitutions are made, it returns **false**.

Optional modifiers: **g** replaces all occurrences of the pattern; **e** evaluates the replacement string as a Perl expression; for the other modifiers, see /*pattern*/ matching. Almost any delimiter may replace the slashes; if single quotes are used, no interpolation is done on strings between the delimiters. Otherwise strings are interpolated as if in double quotes.

If bracketing delimiters are used, *pattern* and *replacement* may have their own delimiters, e.g., **s(foo)[bar]**. If *pattern* is empty, the most recent pattern from a previous successful match or replacement is used.

[$*var* =˜] tr/*searchlist*/*replacementlist*/ [c] [d] [s]

Translates all occurrences of the characters found in the search list into the corresponding character in the replacement list. It returns the number of characters replaced. **y** may be used instead of **tr**.

Optional modifiers: **c** complements the *searchlist*; **d** deletes all characters found in *searchlist* that do not have a corresponding character in *replacementlist*; **s** squeezes all sequences of characters that are translated into the same target character into one occurrence of this character.

pos [*scalar†*]

Returns the position where the last **m//g** search left off for *scalar*. May be assigned to.

study [$var†]

Studies the scalar variable $*var* in anticipation of performing many pattern matches on its contents before the variable is next modified.

File Test Operators

These unary operators take one argument, either a filename or a filehandle, and test the associated file to see if something is true about it. If the argument is omitted, they test $_ (except for -t, which tests **STDIN**). If the special argument _ (underscore) is passed, they use the information from the preceding test or **stat** call.

-r -w -x

File is readable/writable/executable by effective uid/gid.

-R -W -X

File is readable/writable/executable by real uid/gid.

-o -O   File is owned by effective/real uid.

-e -z   File exists/has zero size.

-s   File exists and has non-zero size. Returns the size.

-f -d   File is a plain file/a directory.

-l -S -p

File is a symbolic link/a socket/a named pipe (FIFO).

-b -c   File is a block/character special file.

-u -g -k

File has setuid/setgid/sticky bit set.

-t   Tests if filehandle (**STDIN** by default) is opened to a tty.

-T -B   File is a text/non-text (binary) file. -T and -B return **true** on a null file, or a file at EOF when testing a filehandle.

-M -A -C

> File modification/access/inode-change time. Measured in days. Value returned reflects the file age at the time the script started. See also **$^T** in the section "Special Variables."

File Operations

Functions operating on a list of files return the number of files successfully operated upon.

chmod *list*

> Changes the permissions of a list of files. The first element of the list must be the numerical mode.

chown *list*

> Changes the owner and group of a list of files. The first two elements of the list must be the numerical uid and gid.

truncate *file, size*

> truncates *file* to *size. file* may be a filename or a filehandle.

link *oldfile, newfile*

> Creates a new filename linked to the old filename.

lstat *file*   Like stat, but does not traverse a final symbolic link.

mkdir *dir, mode*

> Creates a directory with given permissions. Sets **$!** on failure.

readlink *expr†*

> Returns the value of a symbolic link.

rename *oldname, newname*

> Changes the name of a file.

rmdir *filename†*

> Deletes the directory if it is empty. Sets **$!** on failure.

stat *file*   Returns a 13-element array (0:$dev, 1:$ino, 2:$mode, 3:$nlink, 4:$uid, 5:$gid, 6:$rdev, 7:$size, 8:$atime, 9:$mtime, 10:$ctime, 11:$blksize, 12:$blocks). *file* can be a filehandle, an expression

evaluating to a filename, or _ to refer to the last file
test operation or **stat** call. Returns an empty list if the
stat fails.

symlink *oldfile, newfile*

Creates a new filename symbolically linked to the
old filename.

unlink *list*

Deletes a list of files.

utime *list*

Changes the access and modification times. The first
two elements of the list must be the numerical
access and modification times.

Input/Output

In input/output operations, *filehandle* may be a filehandle as
opened by the **open** operator, a predefined filehandle (e.g.,
STDOUT) or a scalar variable that evaluates to a reference to
or the name of a filehandle to be used.

<*filehandle*>

In scalar context, reads a single line from the file
opened on *filehandle.* In array context, reads the
whole file.

< >   Reads from the input stream formed by the files
specified in **@ARGV**, or standard input if no arguments were supplied.

binmode *filehandle*

Arranges for the file opened on *filehandle* to be read
or written in binary mode as opposed to text mode
(null-operation on Unix).

close *filehandle*

Closes the file or pipe associated with the filehandle.

dbmclose *%hash*

Deprecated, use **untie** instead.

dbmopen %*hash*, *dbmname*, *mode*
    Deprecated, use **tie** instead.

eof *filehandle*
    Returns **true** if the next read will return end of file, or if the file is not open.

eof   Returns the EOF status for the last file read.

eof( )   Indicates EOF on the pseudo-file formed of the files listed on the command line.

fcntl *filehandle, function,* $*var*
    Implements the *fcntl*(2) function. This function has nonstandard return values.

fileno *filehandle*
    Returns the file descriptor for a given (open) file.

flock *filehandle, operation*
    Calls a system-dependent locking routine on the file. *operation* formed by adding 1 (shared), 2 (exclusive), 4 (non-blocking) or 8 (unlock).

getc [*filehandle*]
    Yields the next character from the file, or an empty string on end of file. If *filehandle* is omitted, reads from **STDIN**.

ioctl *filehandle, function,* $*var*
    Performs *ioctl*(2) on the file. This function has nonstandard return values.

open *filehandle* [, *filename*]
    Opens a file and associates it with *filehandle.* If *filename* is omitted, the scalar variable of the same name as the *filehandle* must contain the filename.

    The following filename conventions apply when opening a file.

    "*file*"   open *file* for input. Also " <*file*".

    ">*file*"   open *file* for output, creating it if necessary.

    ">>*file*"

        open *file* in append mode.

"+<*file*"

> open existing *file* with read/write access.

"+>*file*"

> create new *file* with read/write access.

"+>>*file*"

> read/write access in append mode.

" | *cmd*"

> opens a pipe to command *cmd*; forks if *cmd* is -.

"*cmd* | "

> opens a pipe from command *cmd*; forks if *cmd* is -.

> *file* may be &*filehnd*, in which case the new filehandle is connected to the (previously opened) filehandle *filehnd*. If it is &=*n*, *file* will be connected to the given file descriptor. **open** returns **undef** upon failure, **true** otherwise.

pipe *readhandle, writehandle*

> Returns a pair of connected pipes.

print [*filehandle*] [*list†*]

> Prints the elements of *list*, converting them to strings if needed. If *filehandle* is omitted, prints by default to standard output (or to the last selected output channel, see **select**).

printf [*filehandle*] [*list*]

> Equivalent to **print** *filehandle* **sprintf** *list*.

read *filehandle*, $*var*, *length* [, *offset*]

> Reads *length* binary bytes from the file into the variable at *offset*. Returns number of bytes actually read.

seek *filehandle, position, whence*

> Arbitrarily positions the file. Returns **true** if successful.

select [*filehandle*]

> Returns the currently selected filehandle. Sets the current default filehandle for output operations if *filehandle* is supplied.

---

select *rbits, wbits, nbits, timeout*

> Performs a *select(2)* system call with the same parameters.

sprintf *format, list*

> Returns a string formatted by (almost all of) the usual *printf(3)* conventions.

sysopen *filehandle, path, mode* [, *perms*]

> Performs an *open(2)* system call. The possible values and flag bits of *mode* are system-dependent; they are available via the standard module **Fcntl**.

sysread *filehandle,* $*var, length* [, *offset*]

> Reads *length* bytes into $*var* at *offset*.

syswrite *filehandle, scalar, length* [, *offset*]

> Writes *length* bytes from *scalar* at *offset*.

tell [*filehandle*]

> Returns the current file position for the file. If *filehandle* is omitted, assumes the file last read.

Formats

formline *picture, list*

> Formats *list* according to *picture* and accumulates the result into $^A.

write [*filehandle*]

> Writes a formatted record to the specified file, using the format associated with that file.

Formats are defined as follows:

    format [name] =
    formlist
    .

formlist pictures the lines, and contains the arguments that will give values to the fields in the lines. *name* defaults to **STDOUT** if omitted.

Picture fields are:

@<<<...	left-adjusted field, repeat the < to denote the desired width
@>>>...	right-adjusted field
@| | |...	centered field
@#.##...	numeric format with implied decimal point
@*	a multiline field

Use ^ instead of @ for multiline block filling.

Use ˜ at the beginning of a line to suppress unwanted empty lines.

Use ˜˜ at the beginning of a line to have this format line repeated until all fields are exhausted.

Set $- to zero to force a page break on the next write.

See also $^, $˜, $^A, $^F, $-, and $= in the section "Special Variables."

Directory Reading Routines

closedir *dirhandle*
>Closes a directory opened by opendir.

opendir *dirhandle, dirname*
>Opens a directory on the handle specified.

readdir *dirhandle*
>Returns the next entry (or an array of entries) from the directory.

rewinddir *dirhandle*
>Positions the directory to the beginning.

seekdir *dirhandle, pos*
>Sets position for readdir on the directory.

telldir *dirhandle*
>Returns the position in the directory.

System Interaction

alarm *expr*

Schedules a **SIGALRM** to be delivered after *expr* seconds.

chdir [*expr*]

Changes the working directory. Uses **$ENV{"HOME"}** or **$ENV{"LOGNAME"}** if *expr* is omitted.

chroot *filename*†

Changes the root directory for the process and its children.

die [*list*]

Prints the value of *list* to **STDERR** and exits with the current value of **$!** (errno). If **$!** is 0, exits with the value of **($? >> 8)**. If **($? >> 8)** is 0, exits with 255. *list* defaults to "Died". Inside an **eval**, the error message is stuffed into **$@**, and the **eval** is terminated with the undefined value; this makes **die** the way to raise an exception.

exec *list*

Executes the system command in *list*; does not return.

exit [*expr*]

Exits immediately with the value of *expr*, which defaults to **0** (zero). Calls **END** routines and object destructors before exiting.

fork

Does a *fork*(2) system call. Returns the process ID of the child to the parent process and zero to the child process.

getlogin

Returns the current login name as known by the system. If it returns **false**, use **getpwuid**.

getpgrp [*pid*]

Returns the process group for process *pid* (0, or omitted, means the current process).

---

getppid   Returns the process ID of the parent process.

getpriority *which, who*

    Returns the current priority for a process, process group, or user.

glob *pat*   Returns a list of filenames that match the shell pattern *pat*.

kill *list*   Sends a signal to a list of processes. The first element of the list must be the signal to send (either numeric, or its name as a string). Negative signals kill process groups instead of processes.

setpgrp *pid, pgrp*

    Sets the process group for the *pid* (0 means the current process).

setpriority *which, who, priority*

    Sets the current priority for a process, process group, or a user.

sleep [*expr*]

    Causes the program to sleep for *expr* seconds, or forever if no *expr*. Returns the number of seconds actually slept.

syscall *list*

    Calls the system call specified in the first element of the list, passing the rest of the list as arguments to the call.

system *list*

    Does exactly the same thing as **exec** *list* except that a fork is performed first, and the parent process waits for the child process to complete. Returns the exit status of the child process.

times   Returns a 4-element array (0:$user, 1:$system, 2:$cuser, 3:$csystem) giving the user and system times, in seconds, for this process and the children of this process.

umask [*expr*]

    Sets the umask for the process and returns the old one. If *expr* is omitted, returns current umask value.

---

wait   Waits for a child process to terminate and returns
            the process ID of the deceased process (–1 if none).
            The status is returned in **$?**.

waitpid *pid, flags*

            Performs the same function as the corresponding
            system call.

warn [*list*]

            Prints *list* on **STDERR** like die, but doesn't exit. *list*
            defaults to "**Warning: something's wrong**".

Networking

accept *newsocket, genericsocket*

            Accepts a new socket.

bind *socket, name*

            Binds the *name* to the *socket*.

connect *socket, name*

            Connects the *name* to the *socket*.

getpeername *socket*

            Returns the socket address of the other end of the
            socket.

getsockname *socket*

            Returns the name of the socket.

getsockopt *socket, level, optname*

            Returns the socket options.

listen *socket, queuesize*

            Starts listening on the specified *socket*.

recv *socket, scalar, length, flags*

            Receives a message on *socket*.

send *socket, msg, flags* [*, to*]

            Sends a message on the *socket*.

setsockopt *socket, level, optname, optval*

            Sets the requested socket option.

shutdown *socket, how*

> Shuts down a *socket*.

socket *socket, domain, type, protocol*

> Creates a *socket* in *domain* with *type* and *protocol*.

socketpair *socket1, socket2, domain, type, protocol*

> Works the same as **socket**, but creates a pair of bidirectional sockets.

System V IPC

Depending on your system configuration, certain system files need to be required to access the message- and semaphore-specific operation names.

msgctl *id, cmd, args*

> Calls *msgctl*(2). If *cmd* is **&IPC_STAT** then *args* must be a variable. See the manual for details on the non-standard return values of this function.

msgget *key, flags*

> Creates a message queue for *key*. Returns the message queue identifier.

msgsnd *id, msg, flags*

> Sends *msg* to queue *id*.

msgrcv *id, $var, size, type, flags*

> Receives a message from queue *id* into *var*.

semctl *id, semnum, cmd, arg*

> Calls *semctl*(2). If *cmd* is **&IPC_STAT** or **&GETALL** then *arg* must be a variable.

semget *key, nsems, size, flags*

> Creates a set of semaphores for *key*. Returns the message semaphore identifier.

semop *key, ...*

> Performs semaphore operations.

shmctl *id, cmd, arg*

> Calls *shmctl*(2). If *cmd* is **&IPC_STAT** then *arg* must be a single variable.

shmget *key, size, flags*

> Creates shared memory. Returns the shared memory segment identifier.

shmread *id*, $*var*, *pos, size*

> Reads at most *size* bytes of the contents of shared memory segment *id* starting at offset *pos* into *var*.

shmwrite *id, string, pos, size*

> Writes at most *size* bytes of *string* into the contents of shared memory segment *id* at offset *pos*.

Miscellaneous

defined *expr*

> Tests whether the *expr* has an actual value.

do *filename*

> Executes *filename* as a Perl script. See also **require** in the section "Subroutines, Packages, and Modules."

dump [*label*]

> Immediate core dump. When reincarnated, starts at *label*.

eval { *expr, ...* }

> Executes the code between { and }. Traps runtime errors as described with **eval**(*expr*), in the section "String Functions."

local *variable*

> Creates a scope for the variable local to the enclosing block, subroutine, or **eval**.

my *variable*

> Creates a scope for the variable lexically local to the enclosing block, subroutine, or **eval**.

ref *expr*†

> Returns a **true** value if *expr* is a reference. Returns the package name if *expr* has been blessed into a package.

reset [*expr*]

> Resets ?? searches so that they work again. *expr* is a list of single letters. All variables and arrays beginning with one of those letters are reset to their pristine state. Only affects the current package.

scalar *expr*

> Forces evaluation of *expr* in scalar context.

undef [*lvalue*]

> Undefines the *lvalue*. Always returns the undefined value.

wantarray

> Returns true if the current context expects a list value.

Information from System Files

passwd
Returns ($name, $passwd, $uid, $gid, $quota, $comment, $gcos, $dir, $shell).

endpwent

> Ends lookup processing.

getpwent

> Gets next user information.

getpwnam *name*

> Gets information by name.

getpwuid *uid*

> Gets information by user ID.

setpwent

> Resets lookup processing.

group
Returns ($name, $passwd, $gid, $members).

endgrent

> Ends lookup processing.

getgrgid *gid*

> Gets information by group ID.

getgrnam *name*

> Gets information by name.

getgrent Gets next group information.

setgrent Resets lookup processing.

hosts

Returns ($name, $aliases, $addrtype, $length, @addrs).

endhostent

> Ends lookup processing.

gethostbyaddr *addr, addrtype*

> Gets information by IP address.

gethostbyname *name*

> Gets information by hostname.

gethostent

> Gets next host information.

sethostent *stayopen*

> Resets lookup processing.

networks

Returns ($name, $aliases, $addrtype, $net).

endnetent

> Ends lookup processing.

getnetbyaddr *addr, type*

> Gets information by address and type.

getnetbyname *name*

> Gets information by network name.

getnetent

> Gets next network information.

setnetent *stayopen*

> Resets lookup processing.

services

Returns ($name, $aliases, $port, $proto).

endservent
> Ends lookup processing.

getservbyname *name, proto*
> Gets information by service name.

getservbyport *port, proto*
> Gets information by service port.

getservent
> Gets next service information.

setservent *stayopen*
> Resets lookup processing.

protocols

Returns ($name, $aliases, $proto).

endprotoent
> Ends lookup processing.

getprotobyname *name*
> Gets information by protocol name.

getprotobynumber *number*
> Gets information by protocol number.

getprotoent
> Gets next protocol information.

setprotoent *stayopen*
> Resets lookup processing.

Special Variables

The following variables are global and should be localized in subroutines:

$_   The default input and pattern-searching space.

$.   The current input line number of the last filehandle that was read.

$/   The input record separator, newline by default. May be multicharacter.

`$,`	The output field separator for the print operator.
`$"`	The separator that joins elements of arrays interpolated in strings.
`$\`	The output record separator for the print operator.
`$#`	The output format for printed numbers. Deprecated.
`$*`	Set to 1 to do multiline matching within strings. Deprecated, see the **m** and **s** modifiers in the section "Search and Replace Functions."
`$?`	The status returned by the last `` `...` `` command, pipe **close**, or **system** operator.
`$]`	The Perl version number, e.g., 5.001.
`$[`	The index of the first element in an array, and of the first character in a substring. Default is 0. Deprecated.
`$;`	The subscript separator for multidimensional array emulation. Default is "\034".
`$!`	If used in a numeric context, yields the current value of **errno**. If used in a string context, yields the corresponding error string.
`$@`	The Perl error message from the last **eval** or **do** *expr* command.
`$:`	The set of characters after which a string may be broken to fill continuation fields (starting with ^) in a format.
`$0`	The name of the file containing the Perl script being executed. May be assigned to.
`$$`	The process ID of the Perl interpreter running this script. Altered (in the child process) by **fork**.
`$<`	The real user ID of this process.
`$>`	The effective user ID of this process.
`$(`	The real group ID of this process.
`$)`	The effective group ID of this process.
`$^A`	The accumulator for **formline** and **write** operations.

$^D	The debug flags as passed to Perl using $-D$.
$^F	The highest system file descriptor, ordinarily 2.
$^I	In-place edit extension as passed to Perl using $-i$.
$^L	Formfeed character used in formats.
$^P	Internal debugging flag.
$^T	The time (as delivered by time) when the program started. This value is used by the file test operators $-M$, $-A$, and $-C$.
$^W	The value of the $-w$ option as passed to Perl.
$^X	The name by which this Perl interpreter was invoked.

The following variables are context dependent and need not be localized:

$%	The current page number of the currently selected output channel.
$=	The page length of the current output channel. Default is 60 lines.
$-	The number of lines remaining on the page.
$~	The name of the current report format.
$^	The name of the current top-of-page format.
$|	If set to nonzero, forces a flush after every write or print on the currently selected output channel. Default is 0.
$ARGV	The name of the current file when reading from < >.

The following variables are always local to the current block:

$&	The string matched by the last successful pattern match.
$`	The string preceding what was matched by the last successful match.
$'	The string following what was matched by the last successful match.

$+ The last bracket matched by the last search pattern.

$1...$9...
Contain the subpatterns from the corresponding sets of parentheses in the last pattern successfully matched. **$10** and up are only available if the match contained that many subpatterns.

Special Arrays

@ARGV Contains the command-line arguments for the script (not including the command name).

@EXPORT
Names the methods a package exports by default.

@EXPORT_OK
Names the methods a package can export upon explicit request.

@INC Contains the list of places to look for Perl scripts to be evaluated by the **do** *filename* and **require** commands. Do not modify directly, but use the **use lib** pragma or **-I** command-line option instead.

@ISA List of base classes of a package.

@_ Parameter array for subroutines. Also used by **split** if not in array context.

%ENV Contains the current environment.

%INC List of files that have been included with **use**, **require**, or **do**.

%OVERLOAD
Can be used to overload operators in a package.

%SIG Used to set signal handlers for various signals. **__WARN__** and **__DIE__** are pseudo-signals to attach handlers to Perl warnings and exceptions.

Standard Modules

AnyDBM_File
  Provide a framework for multiple dbm files.

AutoLoader
  Load functions only on demand.

AutoSplit
  Split a package for autoloading.

Benchmark
  Benchmark running times of code.

Carp   Warn of errors.

Config Access Perl configuration information.

Cwd   Get the pathname of current working directory.

DB_File Access to Berkeley DB files.

Devel::SelfStubber
  Generate stubs for a SelfLoading module.

Dirhandle
  Supply object methods for directory handles.

DynaLoader
  Dynamically load C libraries into Perl code.

English Use nice English names for ugly punctuation variables.

Env   Import environment variables.

Exporter
  Implements default import method for modules.

ExtUtils::Embed
  Utilities for embedding Perl in C/C++ applications.

ExtUtils::Install
  Install files from here to there.

ExtUtils::Liblist
  Determine libraries to use and how to use them.

ExtUtils::MakeMaker
  Create an extension Makefile.

ExtUtils::Manifest

Utilities to write and check a MANIFEST file.

ExtUtils::Miniperl

Write the C code for **perlmain.c**.

ExtUtils::Mkbootstrap

Make a bootstrap file for use by DynaLoader.

ExtUtils::Mksymlists

Write linker options files for dynamic extension.

ExtUtils::MM_OS2

Methods to override Unix behavior in ExtUtils::Mak-eMaker.

ExtUtils::MM_Unix

Methods used by ExtUtils::MakeMaker.

ExtUtils::MM_VMS

Methods to override Unix behavior in ExtUtils::Mak-eMaker.

ExtUtils::testlib

Add **blib/*** directories to @INC.

Fatal   Replace functions with equivalents which succeed or die.

Fcntl   Load the C **fcntl.h** defines.

File::Basename

Parse file specifications.

FileCache

Keep more files open than the system permits.

File::CheckTree

Run many filetest checks on a tree.

File::Copy

Copy files or filehandles.

File::Find

Traverse a file tree.

FileHandle

Supply object methods for filehandles.

File::Path
> Create or remove a series of directories.

FindBin Locate directory of original Perl script.

GDBM_File
> Access to the gdbm library.

Getopt::Long
> Extended handling of command-line options. Suits all needs.

Getopt::Std
> Process single-character switches with switch clustering.

I18N::Collate
> Compare 8-bit scalar data according to the current locale.

IO Load various IO modules.

IO::File Supply object methods for filehandles.

IO::Handle
> Supply object methods for I/O handles.

IO::Pipe
> Supply object methods for pipes.

IO::Seekable
> Supply seek-based methods for I/O objects.

IO::Select
> Object interface to the **select** system call.

IO::Socket
> Object interface to socket communications.

IPC::Open2
> Open a pipe to a process for both reading and writing.

IPC::Open3
> Open a pipe to a process for reading, writing, and error handling.

Math::BigFloat
> Arbitrary length float math package.

Math::BigInt

        Arbitrary size integer math package.

Math::Complex

        Complex numbers and associated mathematical functions.

NDBM_File

        Tied access to ndbm files.

Net::Ping

        Check a host for upness.

Opcode   Disable named opcodes when compiling Perl code.

Pod::Text

        Convert POD data to formatted ASCII text.

POSIX   Interface to IEEE Std 1003.1.

Safe   Compile and execute code in restricted compartments.

SDBM_File

        Tied access to sdbm files.

Search::Dict

        Search for key in dictionary file.

SelectSaver

        Save and restore a selected file handle.

SelfLoader

        Load functions only on demand.

Shell   Run shell commands transparently within Perl.

Socket   Load the C **socket.h** defines and structure manipulators.

Symbol   Manipulate Perl symbols and their names.

Sys::Hostname

        Try every conceivable way to get the name of this system.

Sys::Syslog

        Interface to the Unix **syslog**(3) calls.

Term::Cap

        Perl interface to Unix **termcap**(3).

Term::Complete
>	Word completion module.

Term::ReadLine
>	Interface to various readline packages.

Test::Harness
>	Run Perl standard test scripts with statistics.

Text::Abbrev
>	Create an abbreviation table from a list.

Text::ParseWords
>	Parse text into an array of tokens.

Text::Soundex
>	Implementation of the Soundex Algorithm as described by Donald Knuth.

Text::Tabs
>	Expand and unexpand tabs.

Text::Wrap
>	Line wrapping to form simple paragraphs.

Tie::Hash
>	Base class definitions for tied hashes.

Tie::StdHash
>	Basic methods for tied hashes.

Tie::Scalar
>	Base class definitions for tied scalars.

Tie::StdScalar
>	Basic methods for tied scalars.

Tie::SubstrHash
>	Fixed table-size, fixed key-length hashing.

Time::Local
>	Efficiently compute time from local and GMT time.

UNIVERSAL
>	Base class for ALL classes (blessed references).

Environment Variables

Perl uses the following environment variables.

HOME   Used if chdir has no argument.

LOGDIR

   Used if chdir has no argument and **HOME** is not set.

PATH   Used in executing subprocesses, and in finding the
         Perl script if -S is used.

PERL5LIB

   A colon-separated list of directories to look in for
   Perl library files before looking in the standard
   library and the current directory.

PERL5DB

   The command to get the debugger code. Defaults to
   BEGIN { require 'perl5db.pl' }.

PERLLIB

   Used instead of **PERL5LIB** if the latter is not defined.

The Perl Debugger

The Perl symbolic debugger is invoked with **perl -d**.

h   Prints out a long help message.

h *cmd*   Prints out help for the command *cmd.*

h h   Prints out a concise help message.

T   Prints a stack trace.

s [*expr*]

   Single steps.

n [*expr*]

   Single steps around subroutine call.

`RETURN`   Repeats last **s** or **n**.

r   Returns from the current subroutine.

c [*line*]

   Continues (until *line*, or another breakpoint, or exit).

p *expr* Prints *expr.*

l [*range*]

        Lists a range of lines. *range* may be a number, start-end, start+amount, or a subroutine name. If *range* is omitted, lists next window.

w [*line*]

        Lists window around the specified line.

-   Lists previous window.

.   Returns to the executed line.

f *file* Switches to *file* and starts listing it.

l *sub* Lists the named subroutine.

S [!]*pattern*

        Lists the names of all subroutines [not] matching the pattern.

/pattern/

        Searches forward for *pattern.*

?pattern?

        Searches backward for *pattern.*

b [*line* [*condition*]]

        Sets breakpoint at *line*; default is the current line.

b *sub* [*condition*]

        Sets breakpoint at the named subroutine.

d [*line*]

        Deletes breakpoint at the given line.

D   Deletes all breakpoints.

L   Lists lines that have breakpoints or actions.

a [*line*] *command*

        Sets an action for line.

A   Deletes all line actions.

< *command*

        Sets an action to be executed before every debugger prompt.

> *command*

>> Sets an action to be executed after every debugger
>> prompt.

V [*package* [*pattern*]]

>> Lists variables matching *pattern* in a package.
>> Default package is **main**.

X [*pattern*]

>> Like **V**, but assumes current package.

! [[–]*number*]

>> Re-executes a command. Default is the previous
>> command.

! [*pattern*]

>> Re-executes the last command that started with *pat-*
>> *tern.*

!! [*command*]

>> Runs *command* in a sub-process.

H [–*number*]

>> Displays the last –*number* commands.

| *cmd*   Run debugger command *cmd* through the current
   pager.

|| *cmd*   Same, temporarily **selects DB::OUT** as well.

t   Toggles trace mode.

t *expr*   Traces through execution of *expr.*

x *expr*   Evals *expr* in list context, dumps the result.

O [*opt* [=*val*]]

>> Sets or queries values of debugger options.

= [*alias value*]

>> Sets alias, or lists current aliases.

R   Restarts debugger.

q   Quits. You may also use your EOF character.

command

>> Executes *command* as a Perl statement.
